VOL ONE

THE COOKBOOK
FROM BIG MAMA's KITCHEN

Mary Adele Philips, Ph.D.

Recipes to **Soothe the Soul**

THE COOKBOOK: FROM BIG MAMA'S KITCHEN
Recipes to Soothe the Soul
by Mary Adele Philips, Ph.D.

Texarkana, TX 75501-4669
frombigmamaskitchen@gmail.com
1 + (903)-506-7183

Copyright © 2022 by Our Sister Circle
an imprint of Sh'Shares NETWORK, LLC.

All rights reserved. No portion of this publication may be reproduced, distributed, or transmitted in any form or by any means, including photocopying, recording, or other electronic or mechanical methods, without the prior written permission of the publisher, except in the case of brief quotations embodied in critical reviews and certain other noncommercial uses permitted by copyright law.

For permission requests, write to the publisher, addressed
"ATTN: Permissions" at the following:

Sh'Shares NETWORK, LLC
PO BOX 13202
Jacksonville, FL 32206-0202
http://ShShares.com

Discounts are available on bulk orders by associations and corporations for business, educational, and ministry use. For details, contact the publisher at the address above.

ISBN: 978-1-942650-86-7 (Paperback)
ISBN: 978-1-942650-87-4 (Hardcover)

Ladies & Gentlemen,

Humbly, and with extreme pleasure, I am privileged to welcome you to experience a cookbook like none other. This cookbook is one that will excite your taste buds and "wrap you up" within the love of the woman who has diligently written it so that you can partake of these timeless, wonderful treasures of savory foods!

I have known the author for 20 years. I'm honored to be her "Forever 39 Girlfriend," and I'm delighted to say she has blessed my husband and me by cooking in our kitchen – WOW! Dr. Mary Adele Philips is one who can not only cook the best meals – SHE CAN BURN (means she can sho'nuff cook)!

With this cookbook, you can sumptuously feast as she "describes and prescribes" her unique culinary specialties. By now, your mouth should be "watering" as you anticipate preparing each wonderful recipe (aka "prescription"). Get ready to experience: "The Cookbook: From Big Mama's Kitchen" with perfection as you follow her recipes/prescriptions "to the tee!"

It has often been said, "Nothing can bring family and people together like food!" Well, you can indeed expect to experience soulful, soothing, and delicious cooking as you delight yourself, your family, and your friends when you prepare these wonderful meals and desserts.

Get Excited! Get Excited! Get Excited! as you open this "food vault" of love from a wonderful, joyful, MASTER CHEF who intentionally and passionately "LOVES COOKING!" When you prepare these amazing delicacies, remember you are privileged, special, and blessed to savor what is being passed down from generations for YOU and everyone to enjoy and experience!

Blessed and Joyful,
Drs. & Elders Karon & Japhetia Blackwell
JACKSONVILLE, FLORIDA, USA

Where It All Began

There is a tradition in the history of black folks' families that the eldest daughter MUST learn how to cook. No ifs, ands, or buts about it— she HAD to KNOW... HOW TO COOK! My eldest sister, Peggy Elaine, could— and still— can cook! Being fortunate enough to live under the same roof as a Master Chef was a PLUS plus for all of us. Our Maternal-Grandmother, Mrs. Edith Eleanor Dixon Walthall Brown, affectionately known as Miss Elaine, was the greatest cook and the most brilliant and creative teacher of the art of cooking.

I don't know how old Big Sister was when she was drafted into "Miss Elaine's "Boot Camp for Future Chefs," but I was 11. At the tender age of 6, before becoming her newest recruit, I had the privilege of learning how to make cinnamon-sugar-butter toast. Grandmother would boast that I made the best cinnamon-sugar-butter toast in Texas! I would really be grinning from ear to ear because Grandmother was the greatest cook I knew in the whole big ole' entire wide world. If she said I could cook, there was no "bout-a-doubt it" (Grandmother's favorite phrase). I Could Cook! ☺

But, what I did finally come to realize was this, Grandmother was baiting me in! As I grew older, she would be like, "Baby-sister, do you wanna make some money helping me shell this bushel of peas?" I could not say no because she was going to make me do it anyway. ☺ I replied, "Yes, Ma'am," so I could get that lil' ole' piece of change. Some of ya'll out there somewhere reading this, "Ya'll know what I'm talking about!" ☺ Back in the day, four quarters equaled a dollar, and a $1.00 bill was a whole lot of serious "scrilla" (aka...Money)! ☺ I could buy 2 pickles, 3 peppermint sticks, some 2-for-a-penny windmill cookies, and a slice of bologna and still have a few pennies left over! I liked to eat then, and I like to eat now. ☺

As previously stated, I was recruited into "Miss Elaine's Boot Camp for Future Chefs" at the not-so-naïve age of 11. The first thing Grandmother taught me was my way around the kitchen. Which skillet to use for frying chicken and pork chops; which pot to use for frying Buffalo Fish, and the Big Silver Pot to be used for boiling pinto beans or cooking greens in. That pot has been passed down through the generations from her mother's mother, who was my great-great grandmother, then on to her mother, my great-grandmother, and then on to her, Miss Elaine, my grandmother. Miss Elaine passed it on to my mother, who still resides in the land of the living. Mama cooks in it on special occasions. I am so sure one day that Big Silver Pot, along with several other pots, and a huge Cast-Iron Skillet, will be passed on to me.

The very first day of the art of cooking was spent being taught and learning how to make homemade yeast rolls. WOW!! Overwhelming is an understatement! But absolutely delicious was what they turned out to be! That dozen beautiful, perfectly golden-brown yeast rolls afforded me all the confidence I needed to know that if Grandmother instructed me, I could cook anything! ☺

I heard so many great stories of my grandmother's days in the kitchen as the cafeteria cook at St. James Day School and how she cooked in the kitchens of many prominent women in the city of Texarkana. This same grandmother was a Nurse as well. You will "hafta" purchase and read my Memoir (hitting the shelf in 2023) to hear about that aspect of our lives.

Anywho, Grandmother had me laughing out loud and crying real tears at the same time. She told me about how she was preparing a humongous pot of grits for breakfast at St. James Day School, as she had done on many previous mornings. After serving the students and staff the first bowl of grits, it was not long before they returned for a second bowl, and a few returned for a third bowl.

Train up a child in the way he should go: and when he is old,

is was really mystifying to Grandmother as the ildren would barely finish the first bowl of grits orning after morning. When all of the grits had en dipped up, there at the bottom of the pot was e greasy potholder she had looked everywhere r that morning! ☺ Seasoning makes everything ste much better! ☺

One of the most important facets of andmother's art of cooking was this: she was e Queen of Seasonings to Soothe the Soul. andmother's food was so doggone good it would use teeth and tongue to fall out while eating your eal. Her culinary skills would cause you to bite ur own tongue—you would literally chew it up. We children would be trying to hurry and eat erything on our plate so we could eat some more Grandmother's good cooking! Grandmother ver placed a limit on how much a person could t, just as long as the food was not wasted. Her otto, "Waste Makes Want," was what we governed rselves by. Some of us would lick the plate to ep from wasting the crumbs! ☺

The greatest compliment ever paid to my ability cook was stated a few months ago. Big Sister as eating Big Mama's Beef Stew and Cornbread en she looked up at me and stated, "Girl, you n cook! Your food tastes just like Mother's." I felt andmother smile from heaven. I certainly smiled earth.

As an 11-year-old, I wanted to be outside playing th the other children. Instead, I was in the kitchen th Grandmother cooking real food while my ers made mud cakes and rock pies outside. I uld mumble and grumble (but not loud enough Grandmother to hear me) the entire time I was eparing to cook. By the time I finished gathering of the ingredients together to cook the meal, I uld be glad to be in the kitchen doing what I grew love with a purple passion.

In those days, I thought Grandmother was ooooo very mean to have a young girl in the chen cooking what sometimes would be three meals in one day. Today, I am incredibly grateful that Grandmother could see over the horizon to this time when I would be composing a Cookbook for this generation of cooks in our family, along with my extended family of daughters and sons, using recipes passed down through the generations. Grandmother taught me the beautiful, undeniable, delectably delicious art of cooking!

It is with deepest love and affection that I share these recipes and family cooking secrets. I pray that each bite reminds you of how much I love and adore each of you. I am very blessed and fortunate to know you and to have you all in my life!

The Cookbook: From Big Mama's Kitchen is dedicated to the memory of Grandmother's Grandmother: Mama Julia Stafford; Grandmother's Mother: Luphelia Stafford Dixon Fowler; and Grandmother: Edith Eleanor Dixon Walthall Brown (aka Miss Elaine).

I dedicate this cookbook to my Mama, Mrs. Imogene O. Walthall Goodspeed, who still prepares a mean meal in the kitchen!

To all of my daughters, granddaughters, great-granddaughters (someday they will cook from this book too), sisters, nieces, cousins, ForEver39 Girlfriends, sons, brothers, nephews, grandsons, and great-grandsons (someday they will cook from this book as well) and to every person I may never have the privilege of meeting in person; this cookbook was compiled with you in mind. Please prepare each meal utilizing love because it is the single most essential ingredient needed to cook an excellent meal. Enjoy every dish. Savor every moment you spend at the table, breaking bread with loved ones and friends. And please, don't forget to say grace. When you bite into your food, please take a bite for me...cause I did then, and I still do, love to eat! ☺

PS.... If you're interested in "Ms. Elaine's Boot Camp for Future Chefs," let me know, and we can make that happen... I Love you all!

will not depart from it. PROVERBS 22:6

RECIPES

From Big Momma's Kitchen

- 11   Big Mama's Banana Pudding
- 12   Big Mama's Bar-B-Q Chicken
- 13   Big Mama's Oven Bar-B-Que Chicken
- 14   Big Mama's Beef Stew
- 16   Big Mama's Homemade Burgers and Sweet Potato Fries
- 19   Bread Pudding
- 21   Breakfast Omelet (add Veggies and/or Meat)

Fish Friday

- 24   Buffalo Ribs and Backs with French Fried Irish Potatoes and Fried Onions
- 27   Buttermilk Pie
- 29   Big Mama's Cabbage and Collards with Smoked Turkey Necks
- 30   Cabbage and Carrots with Ginger Turmeric Seasoning
- 32   Candied Yams
- 33   Catfish Steaks or Catfish Filets - Fried
- 34   Cheese Ball
- 37   Cherry Cheesecake
- 38   Chicken Enchiladas
- 40   Cinnamon Delight Coffee
- 40   Divinely Delicious Eggs
- 42   Dressing & Chicken Big Mama Style (with Giblet Gravy & Cranberry Sauce)
- 44   Giblet Gravy
- 44   Fire and Ice Pickles
- 45   Big Mama's Hot Water Cornbread
- 47   Jalapeno Poppers
- 48   Big Mama's Meatballs & Spaghetti
- 50   Meat Loaf
- 51   Mexican Cornbread
- 52   Peach Cobbler
- 53   Pork Chops (Fried or Smothered)
- 53   Gravy for Smothered Pork Chops
- 54   Sweet Potato Cake
- 55   Sweet Potato Pie

*Children are a gift from God; they are his reward.
Blessed is the man whose quiver is full.*

PSALM 127: 3-5

Famous Family Recipes

58   Aunt Ollie's 5 Flavor Pound Cake (with Glaze)
60   Mama Julia's Tea Cakes

Aunt Monti Lea Walthall's Recipes

62   Philly Cheese Pound Cake
62   Lemon Caper Chicken Thighs
63   Chicken Enchiladas
64   Puff Pastry Salmon
64   Shrimp Scampi
65   German Potato Salad
66   **Grandmother's Madeira Wine Chicken**

Mama "Imogene" Goodspeed's Recipes

67   Mama Goodspeed's Banana Nut Bread
68   Mama Goodspeed's Chicken Spaghetti
70   Mama Goodspeed's Marinated Vegetables
71   Mama Goodspeed's Pecan Pie
72   Mama Goodspeed's Peanut Butter Cookies
75   Mama Goodspeed's Potato Salad
76   **Neiman Marcus Cookies**

Grace

God is great and God is good.
Let us thank Him for our food.
By His hands, we are fed.
Give us Lord, our daily bread.

AMEN

From Big Mama's Kitchen

Recipes to Soothe the Soul...

BIG MAMA'S
Banana Pudding

45 MINUTES

SHOPPING LIST

- 1 lg. box instant vanilla pudding
- 3 cups cold milk
- 1-8 oz. pkg. cream cheese, softened
- 1-14 oz. can Eagle Brand Milk
- 1 lg. carton Cool Whip
- 1 bag Jackson Vanilla Wafers
- 6 Bananas

DIRECTIONS

Blend pudding and cold milk with mixer, until thick. In separate bowl, mix softened cream cheese and Eagle Brand Milk. Add ½ carton Cool Whip to the mixture. Combine both bowls into one. Slice two bananas and crumble 12 Jackson Vanilla Wafers. Layer the bottom of a glass dish with Jackson Vanilla Wafers. Pour half of pudding mixture over wafers. Add layer of wafers, then a layer of bananas. Pour on remaining mixture. Top with rest of bananas, crumbled wafers and remaining Cool Whip. Refrigerate until ready to serve.

Enjoy!

1 HR 15 MINUTES

BIG MAMA'S Bar-B-Que Chicken

SHOPPING LIST

- 2 whole chickens *(cut into pieces & thoroughly washed)*
- 2 Tbsp garlic powder
- 1 Tbsp salt
- 1 Tbsp black pepper
- 2 Tbsp Worcestershire Sauce
- 2 ½ tsp Cajun seasoning
- 4 garlic cloves
- 1 tsp smoked paprika
- 1/8 tsp shrimp boil *(optional)*
- 1 bell pepper *(sliced)*
- 1 onion
- Sweet Baby Ray's BBQ Sauce

DIRECTIONS

Preheat oven to 400 degrees. Place chicken on foil covered baking pan. Season both sides with spices and Worcestershire Sauce. Place skin side down. Cover with onion, bell pepper and garlic cloves (cut in half). Place pan in oven. Cook for 45 minutes. Turn to opposite side. Cook for additional 15 minutes. Remove from oven. Cover with Sweet Baby Ray's Barbecue Sauce. Increase heat to 450 degrees and allow sauce to become burnished.

Delectably Delicious!

BIG MAMA'S
Oven Bar-B-Que Chicken

1 HR 15 MINUTES

- 2 lbs. bone-in, skin-on chicken pieces
- 1 tsp black pepper
- 1 onion
- 2 Tbsp Olive Oil
- 1 tsp garlic powder
- 3 garlic cloves
- 2 tsp seasoning salt
- 2 Tbsp Worcestershire sauce
- 3 cups Sweet Baby Ray's BBQ Sauce

Preheat oven to 400 degrees. Wash chicken in warm water. Rub each piece with Olive Oil. Season both sides with seasoning salt, pepper, garlic powder, and Worcestershire sauce. Place skin side down on a baking sheet, and roast for 25 minutes. Remove the chicken from the oven and baste with BBQ sauce, a total of three times at 10-minute intervals each.

Increase heat to 425 degrees and cook for an additional 10 minutes. Use brush to baste with BBQ sauce each time. The sauce will thicken and caramelize in the oven. By the time you've added the third layer, you'll have a delicious thick, sweet, sticky layer of BBQ sauce on every inch of the chicken. To get a nice barbeque grill coating, place oven on Broil and observe closely to prevent burning.

Big Mama's Beef Stew

2 HRS 30 MINUTES

- 1 lb. beef stew meat cubes
- 1 tsp salt
- ½ bottle V8 Vegetable Juice
- 1/8 tsp shrimp boil
- 2 lg baking potatoes *(cubed)*
- 2 cups water
- ¼ tsp black pepper
- ¼ cup flour
- 2 ½ cups beef broth
- 2 bay leaves
- 1 bell pepper
- ¼ tsp Meat Tenderizer
- 1 Tbsp garlic powder
- 5 tsp vegetable oil
- 2 beef bouillon cubes
- 1 large onion *(chopped)*
- 1 can baby corn
- 1 can Stewed Tomatoes
- 2 tsp Cajun Seasoning
- ½ cup butter
- ¼ cup Worcestershire Sauce
- 5 med. carrots cut into rounds
- 1 can green beans
- 1 sm can Water Chestnuts

Season beef stew meat cubes with ¼ tsp meat tenderizer and half of the black pepper, salt, garlic powder and Cajun seasoning; 2 tbsp. Worcestershire Sauce and 1/8 tsp shrimp boil in a bowl. Let sit for 2-3 hours (or overnight). Then remove from bowl (do not discard drippings from bowl) and coat with flour mixture consisting of ½ cup flour and remaining black pepper, salt, garlic powder, and Cajun seasoning. Mix well.

Heat vegetable oil. Shake excess flour from stew beef and place in hot oil. Brown both sides, but **do not cook.** Place browned beef in Stew Pot with water, beef broth, 2 Tbsp Worcestershire sauce, onion, bay leaves, butter and drippings from bowl. Bring to a rolling boil. Reduce heat and cook for 30 minutes. Add beef bouillon cubes, V8 Vegetable Juice, potatoes, carrots, and bell pepper. Continue cooking on medium heat for 30 minutes or until potatoes and carrots are soft. Add stewed tomatoes. Drain liquid from cans of baby corn, green beans, and water chestnuts. Add to Stew. Continue cooking on low heat for 30 mins.

Serve with Saltine Crackers, **Mama Goodspeed's Favorite Jiffy Cornbread** or **Big Mama's Hot Water Cornbread**.

Yummy Yum!!

Big Mama's Homemade Burgers

25 MINUTES

SHOPPING LIST

- 2 lbs. ground beef chuck
- ½ cup crushed crackers or bread crumbs
- 1 lg egg
- 2 Tbsp milk
- 2 Tbsp Worcestershire sauce
- 1 tsp salt
- 1 tsp garlic powder
- 1 tsp onion powder
- ½ tsp black pepper

BURGER FIXINS

- Buns, tomatoes, red onion, lettuce, pickles, jalapenos, mayo, mustard

In large mixing bowl add ground beef, crushed crackers or breadcrumbs, egg, Worcestershire sauce, milk, salt, garlic powder, onion powder, and black pepper. Mix by hand until the meat mixture is smooth.

Press the meat into medium round balls. Shape into patties at desired thickness, slightly larger than the buns to account for shrinkage during cooking. Place on cool griddle, skillet or on a baking sheet if cooking in the oven. Press a dent in the center of each patty with a spoon to prevent puffing up as they cook. Separate with a sheet of wax paper if you need to stack the patties. Grill or fry the patties for 3-4 minutes per side or until your desired doneness. Stack the hot patties on hamburger buns, and top with sliced tomatoes, sliced red onions, lettuce, pickles, jalapenos, mayo, and mustard. Serve warm.

Mouth Watering!

& Sweet Potato Fries

 SHOPPING LIST

- 4 sweet potatoes, peeled
- 2 Tbsp Wesson Oil
- 1 tsp garlic powder
- 1 tsp paprika
- 1 tsp salt
- ½ tsp black pepper
- 2 Tbsp corn starch

 DIRECTIONS

35 MINUTES

Preheat oven to 400 degrees.
Cut the sweet potatoes into sticks ¼ to ½ inch wide and 3 inches long. Toss them with oil. Mix the spices, salt, and pepper in a bowl, and toss the sweet potatoes in the seasonings. Then toss into zip lock bag containing corn starch. Lay potatoes flat on baking sheet. Bake about 15 minutes or until brown and crisp on the bottom, then flip and cook about 10 minutes until the other side is crisp. Serve hot. *Note: You may fry in oil or Air Fryer if preferred.*

Delightful!

BIG MAMA'S
Bread Pudding

SHOPPING LIST

- 2 cups cold milk
- ¼ cup butter
- ¼ cup sugar
- 1 tsp ground cinnamon
- ½ tsp ground nutmeg
- ½ tsp salt
- 2 lg eggs *(slightly beaten)*
- 6 cups dry bread cubes *(8 slices bread)*
- ½ cup raisins *(optional)*

40 - 45 MINUTES

DIRECTIONS

Preheat oven 350 degrees.
Heat milk & butter in 2-quart saucepan over medium heat until butter is melted & milk is hot. Mix sugar, cinnamon, nutmeg, salt, and eggs in large bowl. Whisk with a wire whisk until well blended. Stir in bread cubes & raisins (optional). Pour in ungreased 1 ½ quart casserole or baking dish. Bake uncovered 40 to 45 minutes.

SAUCE

- 1 cup brown sugar
- ½ cup butter
- 4 Tbsp brandy extract

Over medium heat, heat all ingredients to boiling in 1-quart saucepan, stirring constantly until sugar is dissolved. Pour over cooked Bread Pudding.

Scrumptious!

BIG MAMA'S Breakfast Omelet

SHOPPING LIST

- 2 lg eggs (per omelet)
- 1/8 tsp salt
- 1/8 tsp black pepper
- 2 tsp milk
- 2 Tbsp butter
- Black olives
- ½ cup shredded cheddar cheese
- Chopped cherry tomatoes
- Minced garlic
- Chopped onions (red, white or spring)
- Sliced jalapeno peppers
- Chopped bell peppers (red or green)
- Mushrooms
- Bacon, ham and/or steak
- Freshly chopped chives

DIRECTIONS

Beat eggs, milk, salt and pepper in small bowl until blended. Heat butter in 6 to 8-inch nonstick omelet pan or skillet over medium heat until hot. Tilt pan to coat bottom. Pour egg mixture into pan. Mixture should set immediately at edges. Gently push cooked portions from edges toward the center with rubber spatula so that uncooked eggs can reach the hot pan surface. Keep the temperature low and slow when cooking the eggs so the bottom doesn't get too brown or overcooked. Tilt pan and gently move cooked portions as needed. When the eggs begin to set, add desired filling but don't overstuff the omelet. Cook for a few more seconds. Fold the omelet in half. Slide it onto a plate with the help of the rubber spatula. Omelet may be topped off with freshly chopped parsley if desired.

10 - 15 MINUTES

So Tasty!

Fish Friday

Very early on Friday mornings, before the rising of the hot Texas Summer Sun, several adults in our village of Steven Courts would go fishing at the Texarkana Dam (**Wright Patman Lake**). Those ladies and gentlemen caught the largest **BUFFALO FISH** our little eyes had ever beheld. The highlight of our day was *scaling and cleaning those fish* in preparation for our Friday evening feast. Sharing good food and much love with our neighbors made the work required of us well worth it! Remembering those days bring tears to my eyes. Grandmother was the best fish fryer *EVER*! I humbly admit that I inherited that gifting and ability from her. My Mother and Sister Kim would proudly co-sign this confession as they enjoy the benefits of the skills I inherited from Grandmother. I can fry a mean batch of **Buffalo Ribs and Backs**. We re-create and celebrate *Fish Friday* just about every Friday in our Mother's home.

It would be remiss of me not to share this gift with each of you. You can do this!! Simply follow the instructions and pray as you prepare the most wonderful meal of the week.... "*Fish Friday.*" While growing up, *Fish Friday* was as close as we came to being Catholic. ☺

Fish Friday Meals...

Growing up as a child in Rose Hill, one of our favorite meals was "Fish Friday."

Buffalo Ribs and Backs with...

4 - 6 MINUTES PER PIECE OF FISH

I recorded most of these recipes as they were written from members of my family. We are from the "country" and do not always speak as others do, so please note: **The Buffalo Ribs and Buffalo Backs in this recipe are pieces of fish.**

- 10 Buffalo Ribs
- 10 Buffalo Backs
- 1 Tbsp Braggs Apple Cider Vinegar
- 3 qt. Wesson Oil
- ¼ tsp shrimp boil
- 1 tsp. pepper
- 1 ½ tsp. garlic powder
- 1 tsp. onion powder
- ¼ tsp salt

Wash fish thoroughly. Soak in water with Braggs Apple Cider Vinegar for 20 to 30 minutes. Heat Wesson Oil to "fish grease hot" in Fry Daddy, deep pot, or deep fryer. Rinse fish and pat dry with paper towels. Rub half of shrimp boil on hands, and then rub on Buffalo Ribs. Rub remaining shrimp boil on hands and then rub on Buffalo Backs. Season fish with pepper, garlic powder, onion powder, and salt if using flour/cornmeal mixture. **DO NOT USE SALT** if using **Louisiana Seasoned Fish Fry** as it will cause fish to be too salty. Place mixture in Ziploc bag and add fish a few pieces at a time. Shake the bag. Once oil is at "fish grease hot" temperature, place fish into oil and let cook for 4-6 minutes. Fish will begin to float to surface once done. Remove from oil and place onto oil-absorbing material, such as a paper towel.

Thank You Grandmother!!

French Fried Irish Potatoes and Fried Onions

15 - 20 MINUTES OR UNTIL GOLDEN

2 - 3 MINUTES

- 6-8 lg Potatoes
- Seasoned Salt
- 1 lg onion
- Fish Grease or cooking oil

Wash potatoes. Peel potatoes and slice in half then quarters. Soak in water for a few minutes. Dab dry with paper towels. Season with Seasoned Salt. Peel onion. Slice into thin circles. Fry in hot Fish Grease or cooking oil once potatoes are done.

Lip Smacking Good!!

Buttermilk Pie

⏱ 55 - 60 MINUTES

SHOPPING LIST

- 1 ½ cup sugar
- ¼ cup flour
- 1 tsp vanilla flavor
- 1 tsp lemon flavor
- 3 eggs *(beaten)*
- 1 cup buttermilk
- ½ cup salted butter
- 1- 9-inch pie crust *(unbaked)*

DIRECTIONS

Preheat oven 350 degrees.
Blend butter, eggs, and buttermilk together. Add flavor. Sift dry ingredients together. Add to mixture. Mix well. Pour into pie crust.
Bake 55 to 60 minutes or until done.

Delectable!

Before!

After!

Big Mama's Cabbage and Collards with Smoked Turkey Necks

3 HRS 45 MINUTES

- 1-2 lbs. smoked turkey necks
- 1 Tbsp meat tenderizer
- 1 Tbsp vinegar
- 1 onion
- ½ green bell pepper
- 2 cloves of garlic
- ½ tsp salt & pepper
- ¼ cup Worcestershire sauce
- 2 lbs. collard greens cut
- 1 large red bell pepper
- 1 tsp garlic powder
- 1 Tbsp minced garlic
- ½ large onion
- 2 tsp seasoned salt
- 1 ½ tsp coarse black pepper
- a pinch of baking soda
- 1 medium head of cabbage
- 1 Tbsp sugar
- 1 Tbsp apple cider vinegar
- 2 Tbsp pure butter

Wash turkey necks thoroughly and soak overnight (if possible) in water with 1 tsp meat tenderizer and vinegar. In the morning, rinse well. Place turkey necks in large boiler. Sprinkle on remaining (2 tsp) of meat tenderizer. Add salt and pepper, Worcestershire sauce, onion, garlic, and bell pepper. Add water to cover at least 2 to 3 inches above turkey necks in boiler. Boil rapidly for 30 minutes. Decrease to medium heat and cook for 1 hour and 30 minutes. Add 2 lbs. washed and cut collard greens, red bell pepper, 1/2 large onion, minced garlic, seasoned salt, black pepper, and garlic powder to pot of turkey necks. Once collard greens begin to boil, add pinch of baking soda to tenderize collard greens. Cook on medium heat for 1 hour and 15 minutes. Cut cabbage in half. Cut the halves in half, then cut into half again. Add cabbage, sugar, apple cider vinegar, butter, and black pepper. Cook an additional 30 to 45 minutes until cabbage is tender.

Enjoyable!!

Cabbage and Carrots with Ginger Turmeric Seasoning

2 HRS 30 MINUTES

SHOPPING LIST

- 1/3 cup pure butter
- 1 ½ med red onions finely chopped *(1 cup)*
- ¼ tsp salt
- 4 garlic cloves, minced
- 2-inch piece fresh ginger, peeled, and minced
- 1 Tbsp ground turmeric
- ½ lb. baby carrots, cut into halves
- 2 lbs. green cabbage, cored and cut into ¾-inch pieces
- ½ cup water

In a large cast-iron skillet, heat the butter. Add chopped onions and salt. Cook over moderate heat, stirring occasionally, until softened, about 5 minutes. Add the garlic, ginger and turmeric and cook. Stir until the vegetables start browning, about 5 minutes. Add the carrots along with water. Cook over moderate heat, stirring, until the carrots are just starting to soften. Stir in the cabbage in large handfuls, allowing the cabbage to wilt slightly before adding more. When all of the cabbage has been added, cover and cook over moderately low heat, stirring occasionally, until the cabbage is tender, 40 to 45 minutes. Serve while hot!

Holy Moly!

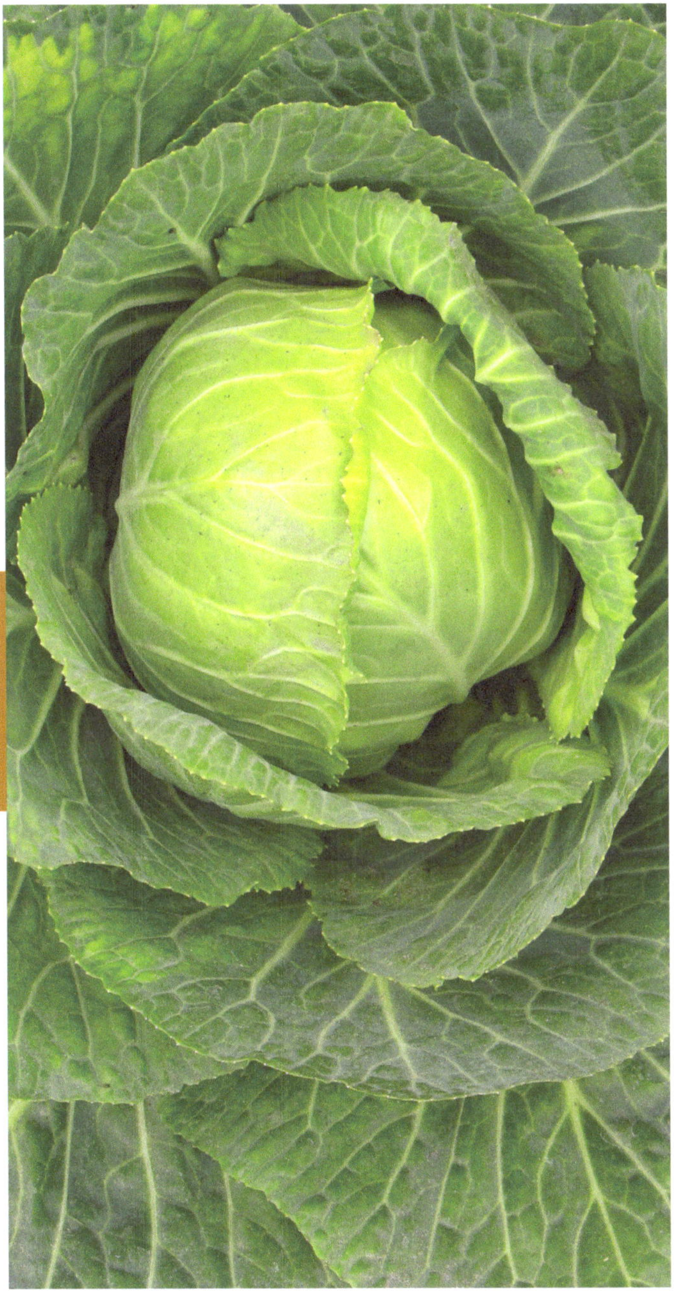

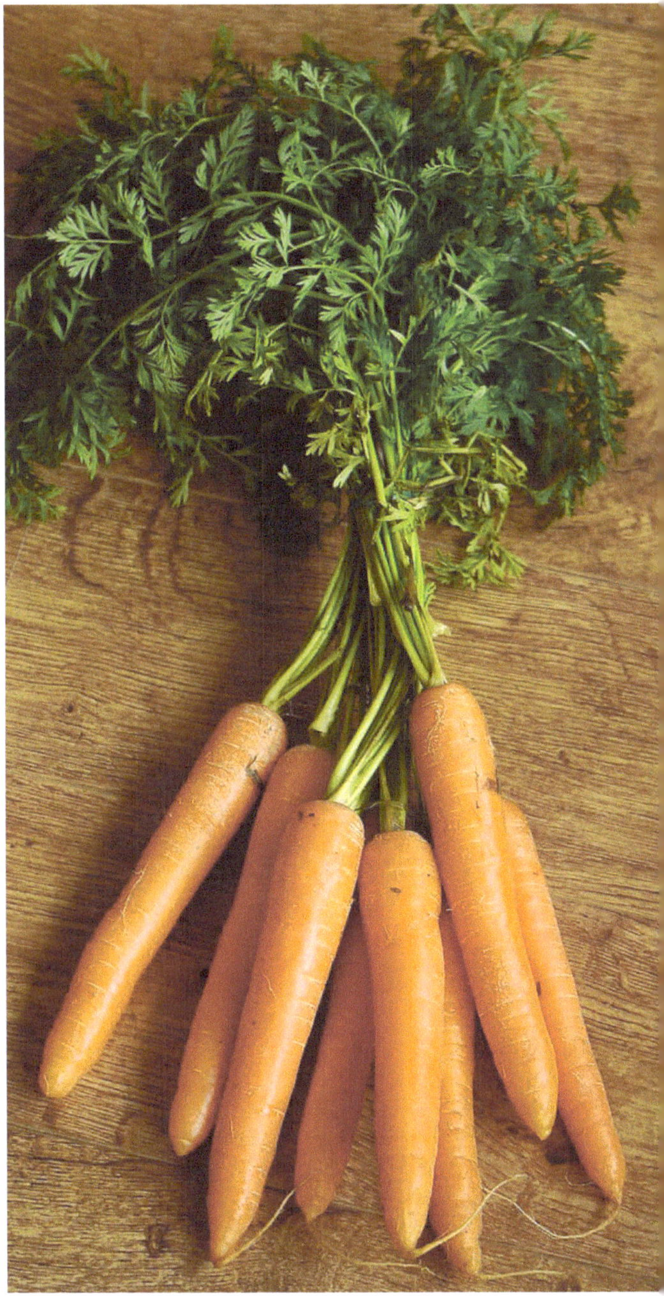

Candied Yams

65 MINUTES

DIRECTIONS

Wash the yams. Peel, then cut into ½ inch thick circles. Place yams, butter, cinnamon, nutmeg, sugar, brown sugar, and vanilla in saucepan. **DO NOT ADD WATER.** Yams produce their own juice. Cook on stovetop at low to medium heat for 30 to 40 minutes or until soft when tested with a fork.

SHOPPING LIST

- 5 medium sized yams
- 1 cup salted butter
- 1 tsp ground cinnamon
- ½ tsp ground nutmeg
- 1 cup granulated sugar
- ¼ cup brown sugar
- 1 Tbsp pure vanilla extract

Ooo Wee!

Catfish Steaks or Catfish Filets, Fried

4 - 6 MINUTES PER PIECE

- 8 Catfish Steaks (bone in) or 8 Catfish Filets
- 3qt. Wesson Oil
- 1 drop shrimp boil
- 1 tsp pepper
- 1 ½ tsp garlic powder
- 1 tsp onion powder
- ¼ tsp salt
- Lemon Juice

Mix 1 ½ cup flour and ½ cup yellow cornmeal or use **Louisiana Seasoned Fish Fry** if preferred for breading fish.

Wash fish well. Heat cooking oil to "fish grease hot" in Fry Daddy, deep pot, or deep fryer. Pat fish dry with paper towels. Rub shrimp boil on hands, and then rub on Catfish. Season fish with pepper, garlic powder, onion powder, and salt if using flour/cornmeal mixture. **DO NOT USE SALT** if using **Louisiana Seasoned Fish Fry** as it will cause fish to be too salty. Place mixture in Ziploc bag and add fish a few pieces at a time. Shake the bag. Once oil is at "fish grease hot" temperature, place fish into oil and let cook for 4-6 minutes. Fish will begin to float to surface once done. Once fish is done cooking, remove from oil and place onto oil-absorbing material, such as paper towel. Squeeze lemon juice as likened or use Louisiana Hot Sauce. **Serve with Sweet Potato Fries or Fried Irish Potatoes and Fried Onions.**

Good!

Cheese Ball

SHOPPING LIST

- 2- 8 oz. pkg. Philadelphia Cream Cheese
- 1- 4 oz. pkg. crumbled blue cheese
- 1- 4 oz. pkg. Shredded Sharp Cheddar Cheese
- 1 small onion, finely chopped (1/4 c)
- 1 Tbsp Worcestershire sauce
- 1 lg garlic clove (finely minced)
- 1/2 cup parsley (fresh or dried)

DIRECTIONS

Place cheeses in medium bowl; let stand at room temperature about 30 minutes or until softened. Beat onion and Worcestershire sauce into cheeses with electric mixer on low speed until mixed. Beat on medium speed 1 to 2 minutes, scraping bowl frequently, until fluffy. Cover and refrigerate at least 8 hours until firm enough to shape into a ball. Shape cheese mixture into 1 large ball. Roll in parsley; place on serving plate. Cover and refrigerate about 2 hours or until firm. Serve with crackers of your choice.

Delicious!

Big Mama's Cherry Cheesecake

SHOPPING LIST

- 1 Graham Cracker Crust (9 inch)
- 1- 8 oz. pkg. cream cheese
- 1 can Eagle Brand Milk
- 1/3 cup Lemon juice
- 1 tsp vanilla extract
- 1 can cherry pie filling

6 HRS 30 MINUTES

DIRECTIONS

Beat cream cheese until light and fluffy. Gradually add sweetened condensed milk and continue beating until smooth and combined. Add lemon juice and vanilla; mix well. Fill graham cracker crust. Refrigerate for 6 hours until set. Top with cherry pie filling before serving.

So Good!

Chicken Enchiladas

1 HR 45 MINUTES

- 8 chicken leg quarters
- 2 onions
- 2 garlic cloves *(chopped)*
- ½ bell pepper Sour Cream
- 2 pkgs. taco seasoning
- 4 lg cans of Enchilada Sauce
- 2 pkg. Sharp shredded cheese
- 1 pkg. Mexican Blend Cheese
- Canola or vegetable oil
- Lg. pkg. yellow corn tortillas
- Picante Sauce
- Sour Cream

Preheat oven to 350 degrees. Boil chicken leg quarters (approximately 30 minutes) with 1 onion, 1 chopped garlic clove and bell pepper. Let cool then debone and remove fat tearing the chicken apart. Mix boiled vegetables along with the chicken and taco seasoning. Place in skillet on medium heat and sauté. Chop remaining onion and mix with finely chopped garlic clove and place to the side. In a small frying pan add about 1 inch of oil. Heat on medium high. Heat enchilada sauce in separate saucepan. Quickly fry tortillas (do not let them get hard – this process should take about 15 seconds for each tortilla). Spray baking pan lightly on bottom and sides. Layer bottom of pan with corn tortillas after browning and dipping in enchilada sauce. Add layer of chicken, sprinkle with onion and garlic mix, and layer with cheeses. Repeat layers and continue process until all ingredients have been used or desired size of Enchilada has been accomplished. After final layer of corn tortillas has been added, spoon remaining enchilada sauce and cheese (if any remains) over top. Cook for 35 minutes in preheated oven or until top layer is golden brown. Remove from oven and let cool about 10 minutes. Cut in serving size squares. Top with picante sauce and or sour cream.

Ooo Wee Delicious!! Ole'

Cinnamon Delight Coffee

20 MINUTES

- 2 heaping Tbsps. Folgers Classic Roast Coffee
- 2 cold 16 oz bottles of water
- 1/8 tsp Ground Cinnamon
- Coffee Creamer of choice; Sugar or Splenda to sweeten

Enjoy!

Pour cold water into Coffee Maker. Add coffee to coffee filter. Sprinkle cinnamon over coffee grinds. Brew. Pour yourself a hot cup of brew when ready. Sweeten and add creamer of choice.

Morning coffee with Mama is one of the highlights of my day!

One morning, I decided to add a little spice to her day. I made coffee and added a hint of ground cinnamon. She loved it!! She said to me, "Girl, whatever you did to this coffee today, keep on doing it! I love the crisp taste! All I need now is a donut!" Thus, began the morning ritual of Cinnamon Delight Coffee.

Try it, won't you? I think you'll "love it" too.

Divinely Delicious Eggs

45 MINUTES

- 6 eggs
- ¼ cup Miracle Whip
- 1 tsp yellow mustard
- 1 Tbsp sweet pickle relish
- 1/8 tsp salt
- 1/8 tsp ground black pepper
- Paprika

*This recipe can be doubled

Place eggs in a single layer in a saucepan and cover with water, 1 ½ inches above the eggs. Boil on medium to high heat for 15 minutes. Remove from heat and leave covered for 5 minutes, then rinse under cold water continuously for 1 minute. Crack egg shells and carefully peel under cool running water. Gently dry with paper towels. Slice the eggs in half lengthwise, removing yolks to a medium bowl, and placing the whites on a serving platter. Mash the yolks into a fine crumble using a fork. Add Miracle Whip, mustard, pickle relish, salt, and pepper, and mix well. Evenly disperse heaping teaspoons of the yolk mixture into the egg whites. Sprinkle with paprika and serve.

Divinely Delicious

Dressing & Chicken Big Mama Style

 CORNBREAD

- 2 Tbsp bacon grease
- 2 cups cornmeal or 1- ½ c cornmeal and ½ cup flour
- 1 tsp baking soda
- 1 tsp salt
- 1 Tbsp sugar *(use only for sweet dressing)*
- 2 lg eggs
- 1 cup Pet Milk
- 1 cup water
- 6 Tbsp unsalted butter, melted

If preferred, you can use Cornbread Mix in the package or Jiffy Cornbread Mix to make bread. Place bacon drippings in a 9 or 10-inch well-seasoned cast iron skillet and put the skillet into the oven. **Preheat oven to 400°F** with the skillet inside. (An uncovered Dutch oven or a metal cake pan can be used if you don't have an iron skillet.) Mix all the dry ingredients together (cornmeal, baking soda, salt, and sugar if using) in a large bowl. In another bowl, beat the egg, milk and water until combined, then mix into the bowl of dry ingredients. Stir in the melted butter. When the oven is hot, take the skillet out. Add the cornbread batter and make sure it is evenly distributed in the skillet. Bake for 20 to 30 minutes, or until golden brown. **Set cornbread aside.**

with Giblet Gravy & Cranberry Sauce

CHICKEN

3 HR 45 MINS TOTAL

- 1 whole chicken or 5 leg quarters
- 5 celery stalks
- 2 lg onions
- 1 bell pepper
- 1 garlic clove
- 1 tsp salt
- 1 tsp pepper
- 1 stick unsalted butter
- Water

Wash chicken thoroughly. Place in large boiler with celery, onions, bell pepper and garlic clove after chopping up. Add salt, pepper and butter. Cover with water. Boil on medium heat high heat for 45 minutes. Let cool. Remove chicken from broth. *Set chicken broth aside.*

DRESSING

- 2 celery stalks
- 1 small onion
- ½ bell pepper
- 2 boiled eggs *(optional)*
- Cornbread
- 3 slices white bread, toasted
- 1 tsp sage
- ½ tsp poultry seasoning
- 3 cups Chicken broth
- ½ bag Pepperidge Farms Herbal Stuffing
- Giblet Gravy
- 1 can Ocean Spray Jellied Cranberry Sauce

Pre-heat oven to 350 degrees. In food processor, place celery, onion and bell pepper. Process until chopped but not to produce juice. In large roasting pan (or any large container) crumble cornbread. Tear and add toast, sage, poultry seasoning and Pepper Ridge Farms Stuffing. Mix thoroughly. Then add processed vegetables. Mix thoroughly once more. Chop and add boiled eggs *if desired*. Start with two cups of chicken broth and mix thoroughly. Pour in more broth to accomplish desired consistency of dressings. Do not get too wet or soupy or leave dressing too dry. **Bake for 1 hour.** Place chicken on cookie sheet and roast until golden brown. *Serve with Giblet Gravy (next page) and Cranberry Sauce.*

Exquisite!

Giblet Gravy

45 MINUTES

- Giblets *(from turkey, or chicken)*
- 4 Tbsp butter
- 4 Tbsp flour
- Salt *(to taste)*
- Pepper *(to taste)*
- 2 cups chicken broth
- 1 cup of water
- 1 can cream of chicken soup
- 2 boiled eggs *(chopped)*

Place giblets in a medium saucepan. Add 1 cup of chicken broth and water. Simmer over low heat until well done. Save any juice left in saucepan. Melt butter in skillet over medium heat. Add flour, salt and pepper, stir occasionally until flour mixture is lightly browned. Chop giblets up and put back into saucepan. Add cream of chicken soup, remaining chicken broth and chopped boiled eggs to skillet. Mix well. Return to saucepan and simmer. Add additional chicken broth if gravy is too thick.

Done!

Fire and Ice Pickles

30 MINUTES

- 1 gal kosher dill pickle spears
- 5 cups sugar
- 6 garlic cloves
- 3 Tbsp crushed red peppers
- 1 Tbsp Tabasco Sauce (optional)

Drain juice from pickles. Put all ingredients into pickle jar, then add pickle spears. Turn for 7 days to mix. On 7th day, place Fire and Ice Pickles in quart jars.

Hot Dog!! Talk about Good!!

BIG MAMA'S
Hot Water Cornbread

 SHOPPING LIST

- 1 ½ cups yellow cornmeal
- ½ cup flour
- 1/8 tsp salt
- 2 Tbsp sugar
- ¼ tsp baking powder
- 1 ½ cups boiling hot water
- ¾ cup Wesson Oil

30 MINUTES

 DIRECTIONS

Place vegetable oil in skillet and heat to hot. Mix cornmeal, flour, salt, sugar, and baking powder together. **DO NOT POUR ALL OF THE WATER IN AT ONE TIME!** To prevent ingredients from getting too wet, pour in a small amount of water at a time. Mixture should be firm but not too dry or too wet. Wet hands with cold water. Form mixture into patties. Fry in hot oil (over medium heat to prevent burning) for 2-3 minutes on each side or until done and golden brown. Remove from oil and place on paper towel lined plate.

My! My! My!

Jalapeno Poppers

SHOPPING LIST

can double recipe

- 1-8oz Philadelphia Cream Cheese
- ½ cup shredded cheddar cheese
- 1 Tbsp Worcestershire Sauce
- 1 garlic clove *(finely minced)*
- Bacon Bits *(Can wrap with Bacon if desired)*
- 12 Jalapeno Peppers

30 MINUTES

DIRECTIONS

Preheat oven to 375 degrees. Wearing disposable gloves, slice the jalapenos in half lengthwise. Scoop out the seeds and membranes. In a bowl mix cream cheese, cheddar cheese, Worcestershire Sauce and garlic. Fill jalapenos with the cheese mixture. Add a few seeds to a portion of cheese mixture to create spicy poppers. Top with Bacon Bits or wrap with bacon. Place on a baking pan and **bake 15-20 minutes** or until golden. If wrapped in bacon, bake until bacon is done. Cool 5-10 minutes before serving.

Ooo La La!

BIG MAMA'S
Meatballs & Spaghetti

⏱ 90 MINUTES

SHOPPING LIST

- 1 lb. Angel Hair Spaghetti
- 1 lb. ground beef
- 1 Tbsp Worcestershire Sauce
- 1/3 cup bread crumbs
- ¼ tsp Italian Seasoning
- ½ cup shredded Parmesan Cheese
- 1 egg
- 2 garlic cloves
- 1/8 tsp salt
- ¼ tsp. black pepper
- 2 Tbsp olive oil
- ½ cup onion
- 1-14 oz. can crushed tomatoes
- 1-14 oz. jar Ragu Old World Sauce
- 1-14 oz. jar Prego
- 2 Tbsp sugar
- 1 bay leaf
- Grated Parmesan Cheese

DIRECTIONS

In a large pot of boiling salted water, cook spaghetti according to package instructions. Drain. Combine beef with Worcestershire Sauce, bread crumbs, Italian Seasoning, shredded Parmesan, egg, minced garlic, salt, and pepper. Mix all ingredients well. Form into 16 balls. In a large pot over medium heat, heat oil. Add meatballs and cook, turning occasionally, until browned on all sides, about 10 minutes. Transfer meatballs to a plate. Add chopped onion to pot and cook until soft for about 5 minutes. Add crushed tomatoes, Ragu, Prego, sugar and bay leaf. Simmer for 30 minutes. Return meatballs to pot and cover. Simmer until sauce has thickened for about 25 – 30 minutes. Serve pasta with a healthy scoop of meatballs and sauce. Top with grated Parmesan Cheese before serving.

Meat Loaf

75 MINUTES

SHOPPING LIST

- 1 ½ lbs. ground beef
- 1 tsp. Worcestershire Sauce
- 1 egg
- 1 chopped onion
- 1 cup milk
- 1 cup seasoned bread crumbs *(or cracker crumbs)*
- 1/8 tsp. garlic powder
- Salt and pepper to taste
- 2 Tbsp brown sugar
- 2 Tbsp mustard
- 1/3 cup ketchup

DIRECTIONS

Preheat oven to 350 degrees.
In a large bowl, combine the beef, Worcestershire Sauce, egg, onion, milk, bread crumbs, garlic powder and season to taste with salt and pepper. Combine the brown sugar, mustard and ketchup and add ¾ of mixture to meat. Place in a lightly greased loaf pan, or form into a loaf and place in a lightly greased baking dish. Pour remaining brown sugar, mustard and ketchup mixture over the meatloaf. Bake for 1 hour.

Delicious!

Mexican Cornbread

- 2 boxes Jiffy corn muffin mix
- 2/3 cup milk
- 2 eggs
- 1-16 oz. can cream style corn
- 1 large onion, chopped
- ¼ cup chopped jalapeño peppers (without seeds)
- 2 cups shredded sharp cheese
- ¼ lb. bacon cooked & crumbled
- ½ lb. turkey or pork sausage cooked & drained
- ½ lb. ground beef cooked & drained
- ½ tsp garlic powder
- ½ tsp chili powder
- Sour Cream

60 MINUTES

DIRECTIONS

Preheat oven to 425 degrees. Coat 9" skillet or pan with cooking spray. Brown hamburger and sausage on medium high heat; drain and dispose of excess grease. Sauté onions in meat; add peppers and bacon; set aside. In a mixing bowl combine jiffy muffin mix, eggs, milk, creamed corn, and garlic and chili powder. Stir to combine; do not over mix. Pour half of batter into prepared skillet. Spread meat mixture over batter. Sprinkle with cheese. Spread remaining batter over cheese. **Bake 30 to 45 minutes or until lightly browned.** Cool 5-10 minutes before cutting. Top with a dollop of sour cream.

Peach Cobbler

- 2 - 16 oz cans Del Monte Freestone Peaches
- ½ cup unsalted butter
- 1 cup all-purpose flour
- ¼ tsp cinnamon
- 2 cup sugar (divided)
- 1 Tbsp baking powder
- 1 cup milk
- Pinch of salt
- 1 Tbsp lemon juice

65 MINUTES

DIRECTIONS

Preheat oven to 375 degrees. Melt butter in baking dish. Combine flour, 1 cup sugar, baking soda & salt. Add milk. Stir. Pour batter over butter. **DO NOT STIR.** Combine 1 cup sugar, lemon juice and peaches and boil over high heat, stirring constantly. Pour over batter. **DO NOT STIR.** Sprinkle with cinnamon. **Bake 40 to 45 minutes or until golden brown.** Serve warm or cold.

Enjoyable!

Pork Chops (Fried or Smothered)

40 MINUTES

- 8-bone in pork chops
- ½ cup flour
- 1 tsp seasoned salt
- ¼ tsp garlic powder
- 1 tsp black pepper
- 1 tsp steak seasoning
- ½ cup Wesson Oil
- 2 Tbsp butter

Rinse pork chops and pat dry with paper towels to remove excess moisture. In a large Ziploc bag, combine flour, seasoned salt, black pepper, steak seasoning, and garlic powder. Place pork chops into the flour seasoning mixture and shake bag to coat evenly. Heat Wesson Oil over medium-high heat in a large skillet and once it is hot, add butter to the skillet. When the butter is melted, cook pork chops 3 to 5 minutes on each side. Place fried pork chop on a plate lined with paper towels to absorb oil. Repeat with remaining pork chops.

Mouth Watering!

Gravy for Smothered Pork Chops
20 MINUTES

Heat oil left in skillet after frying pork chops. Add 2 Tbsp flour mixture (more if needed) used to bread pork chops. On medium heat, stir until flour mixture becomes light to golden brown. Add 1 cup hot water. Stir as gravy is being made. Continue to add hot water until desired consistency of gravy is reached. I recommend making gravy a little thin as it will thicken when pork chops are added. Slice medium onion in circles and add to dish. Cover and simmer on low heat until onions soften. Rice or mashed potatoes are excellent compliments to this dish!

Yum!

Sweet Potato Cake

1 HR 20 MINUTES

SHOPPING LIST

- 2 ½ cups all-purpose flour
- 2 tsp baking soda
- 2 tsp baking powder
- ½ tsp salt
- 1 Tbsp cinnamon
- 2 tsp ginger
- 4 large eggs
- 2 sticks unsalted butter
- 2 cups sugar
- 2 cups Wesson Oil
- 1 Tbsp vanilla extract
- ½ cup finely chopped walnuts
- 3 cups mashed cooked sweet potatoes *(4 sweet potatoes)*

FROSTING

- 1 pkg (8 ounces) cream cheese (softened)
- ½ cup butter (softened)
- 1 tsp vanilla extract
- 2 cups confectioners' sugar (white powdered sugar)

Preheat oven to 350°. Grease cake pans. Whisk flour, baking soda, baking powder, salt, cinnamon and ginger together in a large bowl. In a separate large bowl, beat eggs, butter, sugar, oil and vanilla until well blended. Gradually beat flour blend into egg mixture. Stir in sweet potatoes and walnuts. Pour batter into 2 cake pans or Bundt pan. **Bake at 350 degrees for 40-45 minutes** or until a toothpick inserted in center comes out clean. Cool completely in pan on a wire rack. Pour onto cake plate. In a small bowl, beat cream cheese, butter and vanilla until blended. Gradually beat in confectioners' sugar until smooth. Spread over cooled cake.

Pleasantly Sweet!

Sweet Potato Pie

2 HRS 10 MINUTES

SHOPPING LIST

- 2 lg. Sweet Potatoes
- 1 stick butter
- ¾ cup white sugar
- ½ cup brown sugar
- ½ cup brown sugar
- ½ cup Carnation Evaporated Milk
- 2 eggs
- ½ tsp nutmeg
- ½ tsp cinnamon
- 1 tsp vanilla extract
- 1-9-inch unbaked pie crust

DIRECTIONS

Preheat oven to 350 degrees. Boil sweet potatoes whole, in skin, for 45 to 55 minutes. Sweet potatoes are done when fork or toothpick slides through them easily. Run cold water over the potatoes and remove the skin. Break apart potatoes in a bowl. Add butter and mix well with mixer. Stir in white and brown sugar, milk, eggs, nutmeg, cinnamon and vanilla. Beat on medium speed until mixture is smooth. Pour filling into an unbaked pie crust. **Bake for 55 to 60 minutes**, or until toothpick inserted in center comes out clean. Pie will puff up and then will sink down as it cools.

Flavorsome!

AUNT OLLIE'S 5 Flavor

SHOPPING LIST

- 1 cup butter *(at room temperature)*
- ½ cup Crisco Shortening
- 3 cups sugar
- 6 lg eggs
- 3 cups all-purpose flour
- ½ teaspoon baking powder
- ¼ tsp salt
- 1 cup whole milk
- 1 tsp vanilla extract
- 1 tsp almond extract
- 1 tsp coconut extract
- 1 tsp rum extract
- 1 tsp butter extract

1 HR 40 MINUTES

Preheat oven to 325° F. Coat a 10-inch tube pan or Bundt pan with Crisco shortening and sugar. With mixer, cream butter, shortening, and sugar until fluffy in bowl. Stop mixer and scrape sides. Mix again. Add eggs **one at a time** beating each one in before adding the next. Stop mixer and scrape sides. Mix again. Add the extracts to the milk. Sift the flour, salt and baking powder together. Alternate: add a portion of the flour mixture; then add portion of milk mixture to the creamed sugar mixture beginning and ending with the flour. Stop the mixer and scrape the sides of the bowl. Mix until well blended. Pour batter into the prepared cake pan. Smooth the top. **Bake for 75 to 85 minutes or until done.** Carefully insert a toothpick into the center of the cake. The cake is done when dry crumbs or no crumbs stick to the pick.

Pound Cake

30 MINUTES

 SHOPPING LIST

GLAZE
- ½ cup sugar
- ¼ cup butter
- 1 Tbsp water
- ½ tsp vanilla extract
- ½ tsp almond extract,
- ½ tsp coconut extract
- ½ tsp rum extract,
- ½ tsp butter extract

At the **70 minute** mark of the cake baking, prepare the glaze. In a small saucepan over medium heat, whisk together the sugar, butter, and water. Bring to a slow boil, reduce heat, and simmer for three minutes, whisking about every 30 seconds. Remove the pan from the heat and whisk in the extracts. When the cake is done cooking, remove from the oven and use a long skewer to poke holes all over the cake while it is still in the pan. Loosen the cake around the edges of the pan as well as the center hole with a butter knife. Carefully pour the hot glaze over the cake allowing the glaze to seep into the cake. Allow the cake to set 10 to 15 minutes to soak in the glaze. Once the glaze has been absorbed, loosen the edges and center of the cake again using a butter knife. Flip cake over onto a cake platter. Store in an airtight cake plate either on the counter or in the refrigerator. It will stay fresh on the counter 3 to 4 days and in the refrigerator 5 to 7 days.

Thanks Aunt Ollie...

MAMA JULIA'S Tea Cakes

25 MINUTES

SHOPPING LIST

- ¼ cup butter
- 1 ¾ cups sugar
- 2 eggs
- 1 tsp vanilla extract
- 3 cups flour
- ½ tsp baking soda
- ½ tsp salt
- ¼ tsp ground nutmeg

DIRECTIONS

Preheat oven to 325. In a medium bowl, cream together butter and sugar until smooth. Beat eggs in one at a time, stir in vanilla. Combine flour, baking soda, salt, and nutmeg; stir into the creamed mixture. Knead dough for a few turns on a floured board until smooth. Cover and refrigerate until firm. On a lightly floured surface, roll the dough out to ¼ inch in thickness. Use a Mason jar to cut perfectly round Tea Cakes. Place Tea Cakes 1 ½ inches apart on baking sheet to prevent sticking together while cooking. Bake for 8 to 10 minutes in the preheated oven. Allow Tea Cakes to cool on baking sheet for 5 minutes before removing.

Delightfully Delicious!

Aunt Monti Lea Walthall's Recipes

Delectable!

Philly Cheese Pound Cake

⏱ 1 HR 40 MINUTES

- 8 oz. Philly cream cheese
- 3 sticks butter
- 3 cups sugar
- 6 eggs
- 1 tsp vanilla extract
- 1 tsp any other flavoring you like
- 3 cups flour *(sifted)*

Preheat oven to 350 degrees. Mix/beat cream cheese, butter and sugar until very smooth. Add in eggs, vanilla and additional flavoring of your choice, and beat until smooth. Mix in flour a little at a time. Bake until done (about 1 hr. 40 minutes). Let cool 10 minutes and remove from pan.

Lemon Caper Chicken Thighs

⏱ 30 - 40 MINUTES

- ½ cup all-purpose flour
- Black pepper
- Salt
- 4 skinless boneless chicken thighs (trimmed of all fat)
- 2 Tbsp vegetable oil
- 1 cup chicken broth
- Juice of 1 fresh lemon
- Chopped fresh parsley
- Lemon peel from 1 lemon sliced very thinly
- 2 Tbsp capers, drained

Combine flour, salt and pepper on sheet of wax paper. Coat chicken with flour mixture. Heat oil in large skillet over medium heat. Add chicken to skillet and cook, turning once until browned and cooked through (about 10-15 minutes). Transfer chicken to a plate. Add sliced lemon and remaining flour to skillet cooking until well mixed (about 5-10 minutes). Add broth, lemon juice and capers to skillet reducing (thickening) broth slightly. Return chicken to skillet and spoon some of the broth/caper/lemon peel mixture on top of each chicken thigh. Cover and reduce heat to low and simmer until chicken is heated through (about 5 minutes). Sprinkle with parsley. Serve chicken drizzled with lemon peel/caper sauce.

Chicken Enchiladas

1 HR 30 MINUTES

SHOPPING LIST

- 8 chicken leg quarters
- 1 onion
- 1 can cream of chicken soup
- 1 can cream of mushroom soup
- Corn tortillas
- Chopped green chilies
- Mozzarella cheese shredded
- Vegetable oil

DIRECTIONS

Preheat oven to 350 degrees. Boil chicken leg quarters (approximately 30 minutes). Let cool then debone and remove fat tearing apart the chicken into strips. Chop onion and add to chicken with 2 Tbsp oil. Simmer for approximately 20 minutes to cook onions. Add cream of chicken and mushroom soups to chicken. Use ½ can of water to get remaining soups out of can and add to pan. Season as desired with salt and pepper. Let simmer for approximately 30 minutes until hot. Spray baking pan lightly on bottom and sides.

In a small frying pan add vegetable oil to about 1 inch. Heat on medium high. Quickly fry tortillas (do not let them get hard – this process should take about 15 seconds for each tortilla). Layer baking pan with some of the chicken/soup mixture, then tortillas, add chilies (if desired) and cover layer with mozzarella cheese. Continue layering until you have used all chicken/soup mixture. Final layer will be mozzarella cheese. Use as much or as little cheese in each layer as you desire. **Cook for 35 minutes or until top cheese layer is golden.** Remove from oven and let cool about 10 minutes. Cut in serving size squares.

Puff Pastry Salmon

45 MINUTES

- 2-12-ounce skinless boneless salmon filets
- Seasoned salt to taste
- ½ tsp garlic powder
- 1 tsp onion powder
- 1/3 cup Basil pesto
- 1 (6 oz) package spinach leaves
- 1 package frozen puff pastry (box will contain two pastry squares)

Preheat oven to 375. Season salmon fillets with salt, garlic powder and onion powder. Divide ½ of the spinach between the two sheets (squares) of puff pastry. Place a salmon fillet on top of each mound of spinach. Spread the pesto on the salmon fillets and top with remaining spinach. Moisten the edges of the puff pastry with water, fold to center and seal the seams. If you like more spinach, use more spinach – the more used the more challenging it will be to fold the pastry to center and seal the seams. B**ake in preheated oven for 20-25 minutes** until the pastry is puffed and golden and salmon has cooked all the way through.

Shrimp Scampi

20 MINUTES

- 1 ½ lbs. jumbo shrimp (shelled & deveined)
- Kosher Salt (to taste)
- Fresh ground black pepper (to taste)
- 2 tbsp. unsalted butter
- 2 tsp minced garlic
- ¼ cup dry Vermouth wine
- 1 tbsp. fresh lemon juice
- 2 tsp finely chopped flat-leave parsley
- ¼ tsp grated lemon zest

Combine everything except shrimp in saucepan cooking together until well mixed. Add shrimp. **Cook for 5 minutes.** Serve over noodles, angel hair pasta.

German Potato Salad

1 HR 25 MINUTES

SHOPPING LIST

- 1 onion
- 12 oz. bacon
- 8-10 lg russet potatoes
- ¾ cup mayonnaise
- ¾ cup sour cream
- ½ to ¾ cup dill relish
- Seasoned salt
- Ground pepper
- 4 eggs (boiled, peeled and shredded)

DIRECTIONS

Pre-heat oven to 325 degrees. Chop onion and bacon and cook together in skillet until bacon is crisp. Do not drain, set aside. Boil potatoes (with jacket/peel on) until cooked (a fork goes through the potato with little resistance). Let cool, then peel and cube. Add to potatoes the mayonnaise, sour cream, relish, salt/pepper (to your taste) and mix well. Do not cream the potatoes. Reheat bacon and onions until hot and add to potatoes (add the grease from the bacon as well). Mix together. Finally, add the shredded eggs and mix well. **Cook in oven approximately 30 minutes – do not cover.**

Schmeckt So Gut!
("Tastes So Good" in German)

GRANDMOTHER'S Madeira Wine Chicken

 SHOPPING LIST

- 1 lb. chicken breasts skinless (4-6)
- ½ tsp salt
- ½ tsp pepper
- ½ tsp garlic powder
- 3 Tbsp Wesson Oil
- 2 cloves garlic (minced)
- 1 lb. Baby Bella Mushrooms cleaned and sliced
- 1 cup chicken broth
- 2 cups Madeira Wine
- 1 Tbsp all-purpose flour
- 2 Tbsp butter

40 MINUTES

 DIRECTIONS

Wash chicken breast thoroughly and season with salt and pepper. Heat 2 Tbsp Wesson Oil in a large skillet or a saucepan over medium-high heat. Add the chicken breasts to the skillet and cook for about 3 to 4 minutes on each side until golden brown. Remove the chicken breasts from the skillet and set aside. Add the remaining 1 Tbsp of Wesson Oil to the skillet and add the Baby Bella Mushrooms. Season the mushrooms with garlic powder. Cook for about 8 minutes until the mushrooms start to brown. Stir occasionally. Add garlic, Madeira wine and chicken broth to the skillet and stir. Reduce heat and cook for another 15 minutes until the sauce thickens a bit. To thicken the sauce more, take a ¼ cup of the liquid from the pan and whisk it with one tablespoon of flour, then pour it back into the saucepan and stir. The sauce should thicken almost instantly. Add the butter and stir. Add the chicken breasts back to the pan and cook for another 5 minutes.

Quite Appetizing!

MAMA GOODSPEED'S
Banana Nut Bread

60 MINUTES

SHOPPING LIST

- 3 cups flour
- 1 ½ tsp salt
- 1 ½ tsp baking soda
- 1 ½ cups sugar
- ¾ cup butter
- 1 ½ tsp vanilla extract
- 4 eggs
- 4 bananas (very ripe)
- ¾ cup chopped nuts

DIRECTIONS

Sift flour, salt, and soda together and mix with nuts. In separate bowl, cream butter, sugar and vanilla together. Beat eggs in **one at a time**. Mash bananas and add to creamed mixture. Blend all ingredients thoroughly. Pour into loaf pans. **Bake at 350 degrees for 45 minutes.**

Delicious with Cinnamon Delight Coffee!

MAMA GOODSPEED'S
Chicken Spaghetti

35 - 45 MINUTES

SHOPPING LIST

- 1 lg. chicken or 6 chicken quarters
- 1 lg. onion
- 2 stalks celery
- 1 tsp garlic powder
- 1 tsp onion powder
- 1-10 oz. can RoTel Tomatoes
- 2-10.5 oz. cans cream of mushroom soup
- 1-16 oz. pkg. Velveeta Cheese
- 4 oz. Cream cheese
- 1 cup shredded sharp cheddar cheese
- 1-16 oz. pkg. spaghetti

DIRECTIONS

Preheat oven to 350 degrees. Slow cook chicken with onions and celery. Cook over medium-low heat until done. Try not to boil the chicken as it can make it tough. Allow to cool enough to handle. Then debone and shred using two forks. Lightly grease a 13x9-inch baking dish with nonstick cooking spray. Cook spaghetti according to the package directions. Drain and set aside. In a large pot, combine the RoTel with the juice, undiluted cream of mushroom soup, Velveeta cheese, and cream cheese. Cook over low heat stirring constantly with wooden spoon until the cheeses have melted. Add the garlic powder and onion powder. Add the shredded chicken and cooked spaghetti. Mix well. Pour the mixture into the baking dish and sprinkle with the shredded cheddar cheese. **Bake for 20 to 30 minutes** or until heated through and the cheese has melted.

Ahhhhh! Amazing!

MAMA GOODSPEED'S
Marinated Vegetables

24 HRS 15 MINUTES

SHOPPING LIST

- 1 can LeSUEUR sweet peas (drained)
- 1 can French style green beans (drained)
- 1 onion (chopped)
- 1 bell pepper (chopped)
- 1 small jar pimentos
- 1 cup chopped celery
- 1 cup sugar
- 1 cup vinegar
- ½ cup Wesson Vegetable Oil

DIRECTIONS

Mix peas with beans, onion, bell pepper, pimentos, and celery. Mix sugar, vinegar, and oil together. Pour over vegetables. **DO NOT COOK.** Marinate in refrigerator for 24 hours. Serve cold.

Appetizing!

MAMA GOODSPEED'S
Pecan Pie

1 HR 15 MINUTES

SHOPPING LIST

- 1 cup white corn syrup
- 1 cup dark brown sugar
- 1/3 tsp salt
- 1/3 cup melted butter
- 1 tsp. vanilla flavor
- 3 eggs
- 1 cup pecan halves
- 1- 9-inch-deep dish pie crust (unbaked)

DIRECTIONS

Mix corn syrup, brown sugar, salt, butter, vanilla flavor and eggs using large mixing spoon. **DO NOT USE MIXER.** Pour mixture into pie crust and top with pecans. ***Bake at 350 degrees for 45 minutes to 1 hour.*** Observe closely as cook time varies.

Heavenly!

Mama Goodspeed's Peanut Butter Cookies

23 MINUTES

🛒 SHOPPING LIST

- ½ cup Crisco shortening
- ½ cup peanut butter
- 1/3 cup white sugar
- 1/3 cup brown sugar
- 1 egg
- 1 tsp vanilla extract
- 1 ½ cup flour
- 1 tsp salt
- 1 tsp baking powder

DIRECTIONS

Cream the shortening and peanut butter together. Beat in white sugar and brown sugar, one at a time. Add egg and vanilla extract. Beat well with mixer. Sift flour, salt and baking powder. Add to mixture, blending thoroughly. Shape into balls. Place on cookie sheet and flatten with a fork. **Bake at 350 degrees for 18 minutes.**

Delectable!

MAMA GOODSPEED'S Potato Salad

45 MINUTES

SHOPPING LIST

- 1 lb. Russet potatoes
- ½ cup sweet onions
- ¼ cup sweet pickle relish
- 3 boiled eggs
- ¼ celery stalk
- ¾ c Miracle Whip
- 1 Tbsp yellow mustard
- 1 Tbsp sugar
- Salt and pepper to taste

DIRECTIONS

Wash, peel and dice potatoes into ½ inch cubes. Place potatoes in a large deep pot with enough water to cover potatoes and season with salt and pepper. Boil until the potatoes are tender to the bite. Check often, because you don't want potatoes to get mushy. Drain potatoes when done. Peel the eggs. Place the egg yolk of 1 egg in a large bowl and mash. Dice the egg white of the same egg and place it into the bowl. In large bowl mix and stir onions, relish, finely diced celery, Miracle Whip, mustard and sugar together to form a sauce. Stir in cooled potatoes until potatoes are coated in the sauce. Gently mash a few of the potatoes, while stirring to create a creamier, thickened texture. Add more salt and pepper to taste if needed. Slice remaining boiled eggs and use to garnish salad. Sprinkle lightly with paprika. Refrigerate.

Neiman-Marcus Cookies

 25 MINUTES

SHOPPING LIST

- 5 cups oatmeal
- 4 cups flour
- 2 tsp baking soda
- 1 tsp salt
- 2 tsp baking powder
- 2 cups butter
- 2 cups sugar
- 2 cups brown sugar
- 4 eggs
- 2 tsp vanilla extract
- 24 oz chocolate chips
- 1-8 oz. Hershey Chocolate Bar (grated)
- 3 cups chopped nuts

DIRECTIONS

Blend oatmeal in a blender to a fine powder. Mix in flour, baking soda, salt and baking powder. In a large mixing bowl, cream together butter, sugar and brown sugar. Add eggs and vanilla. Blend in oatmeal flour mixture. Add chocolate chips, Hershey bar and nuts. Roll into balls and place 2 inches apart on a cookie sheet. **Bake at 375 degrees for 10 minutes.**

*Makes 112 cookies. *(You may use half of recipe for fewer cookies.)*

www.ingramcontent.com/pod-product-compliance
Lightning Source LLC
Chambersburg PA
CBHW042048120526
44592CB00030B/26